More Reflections on Faith

Campbell Miller

Meditations in the Form of Conversations with God

www.fast-print.net/store.php

MORE REFLECTIONS ON FAITH
Copyright © Campbell Miller 2013

The right of Campbell Miller to be identified as the author of this work has
been asserted by him in accordance with the Copyright, Designs and
Patents Act 1988 and any subsequent amendments thereto.

A catalogue record for this book is available from the British Library

ISBN 978-178035-720-1

First published 2013 by
FASTPRINT PUBLISHING
Peterborough, England.

For Isabel
The memory of whose quiet faith
and loving companionship
is still a source of joy and comfort

Acknowledgements

Once again, I am grateful to my good friends,
June Jones and Keith Evans for their willingness to read and comment
on my first draft of these Reflections and for their encouragement to
publish.

I also express my gratitude again to the Congregation of St
Columba's United Reformed Church, Wolverhampton, whose warm
friendship and fellowship for the past 18 years has been a constant
source of inspiration and support to me

Contents

Introduction

The meditations in my previous book, "Reflections on Faith", developed as I found myself, almost unconsciously, relating to God, in the light of my faith, the many thoughts which arose in my mind through the various experiences which life brings. Some of them arose from distressing events such as the loss of my wife: others from quietly reflecting on aspects of Christian belief and practice and my continuing involvement in the on-going life and worship of a Church community

In this second book, I have included more meditations in the same style as before - in the form of conversations with God. I have given expression to my thoughts or questions addressed to God and I have reflected on what kind of answer God might give! I freely admit, as I said in my first book, that the responses from God which I have included, may sometimes reflect what I would like to hear! But I have tried to be as honest as I can be and the answers do emerge from pondering what I have come to believe after many years of being a Christian.

A substantial part of this book is made up of meditations relating to the Apostle's Creed. I have a problem with creeds! Of course they serve a very useful purpose in setting out what are regarded as the main tenets of the Christian faith. But I am suggesting that we ought to reflect on the meaning of each of these statement of belief and ask ourselves "do I really believe that?" I see this as an important part of being honest and mature about our faith. I find it very sad, though perhaps inevitable, that the essential message of Jesus about love - God's love for us and our love for one another – has so often developed into a system of dogma which are supposed to be believed if we are to be regarded as true Christians That is why I have engaged in these 'conversations with God' about the creed. I do not expect universal agreement with the points of view which I have expressed – I do hope, however, that honest reflection and clearer understanding of what one believes will result!

Another section of this book is made up of meditations on the Lord's Prayer. These arose from a feeling I have that every time I recite these words in worship, I am not taking them seriously – the words roll off my tongue so easily: I feel they are too familiar to me, after years of this being a part of worship, and I suspect that often others in the congregation are doing the same. It is my hope that these meditations may help others to find this wonderful prayer which is at the heart of Christian worship all over the world, more meaningful and more relevant to their lives.

The other meditations are on a variety of issues which have arisen in my mind at various times, governed, I suppose, by such factors as - how I have been feeling, what has been going on around me, news items which have set me thinking, what I have been reading, and so on. I find it helpful to sit down and reflect quietly, trying to relate my thoughts and questions to my faith, which is important to me It is my hope that others may find something from these meditations which helps their faith and encourages them to embark on their own, meaningful conversations with God.

Lord, I want to be sure...

Lord, I have often been asked,
"How can I be sure about God?"
There are times when
I have asked the same question myself!
Living in this increasingly materialistic society,
it is much easier to trust
what can be seen and handled –
perhaps it is just being human to want proof!
I remember, when at school, being intrigued
by geometric theorems in which,
proof was worked out that a statement,
for example, about a triangle was true -
"in a right angled triangle, the square on the hypotenuse
is equal to the sum of the squares on the other two sides."
(I find it amazing that I still remember that!)
Is it wrong to wish at times for a similar kind of proof
for the reality of your existence
even when I know that there is none?
Those of us who take belief in you seriously
seem to be in a minority.
Some regard us with rather light-hearted pity,
as if to say, "how can you be so foolish to believe
in a loving God, since we all live in a world

which contains so much evil and pain?"
There are others who envy us,
wishing that they could believe but somehow,
find it too difficult.

Lord, am I foolish to go on believing in you,
a divine being who is supposed
to be loving and caring towards his world?
If inexplicable tragedy
should come to me and my family,
should I still hold on to my faith?
Am I foolish to go on celebrating Easter with the
resurrection of Jesus at the heart of it,
when reason suggests that
such events which defy the laws of nature
really do not happen?
I must confess that faith is not always easy!

Of course it would be so much easier
if I could see you!
One day my faith is strong and secure
and I am glad to have these conversations with you,
but the next it seems somewhat frail:
one day I feel quite certain that you are there,
listening to me and responding to me
in the quietness of my mind -
the next, I am not so sure.

Is it that my circumstances have changed
and the faith I thought was strong,
is being put to the test?
I suppose this is how Job felt when he cried out,
"O that I knew where I might find Him".
But he, in spite of his doubts,
continued to reach out with faith to you,
the invisible God.
I know I must persist in translating my belief
into action and continue to reach out
and find, again and again, the satisfying
response of your loving presence.
Lord, help me

My child, I am not some mathematical proposition
which follows the rules of logic.
When you consider matters of the spirit,
you have moved outside the realm
of what can be proved and disproved -
there can be no such thing as proof.
Some may point to the wonder
and beauty of the world,
directing you to the order and pattern
in which it is sustained;
they may point to the vastness of the universe,
a vastness which is virtually impossible
to comprehend with a human mind.

None of that is proof that I am real!
It is by faith alone that I am known.
As I have reminded you
in some of our previous conversations,
doubt is not the opposite of faith -
doubt is faith struggling.

Wishing for proof does not offend me.
It shows an honest desire to know me!
Continue on your pilgrimage of faith –
that path will surely lead you closer to me.
Mine are the feet which follow you,
even on your darkest days of doubt.
Mine are the hands which reach out,
waiting for you to grasp them
when you are in danger of falling.
Mine is the quiet, loving voice which encourages you
when you are feeling sad and lonely.
Be assured, I will never let you down!

Lord, life is a mystery...

Lord, I remember, as a young minister,
considering the suggestion that,
while it is human to ask all sorts of questions
about life and its experiences,
there are really three basic questions
which lie at the heart of all our search for meaning –
"Who am I?
Why am I here?
Where do I go when I leave here?"
I also remember preaching a sermon on each question -
I cannot recall what I said,
but I am sure it would be different
from what I would say now, in the light of
years of reflecting on life's experiences
and relating my faith to them!

Awareness of mystery lies behind the questions –
the mystery of life,
the mystery of our individual identity,
the mystery of love
the mystery of death,
and, of course,
if we have come to some belief in you -
the mystery of your eternal being,

Why am I here?
Has my life any real purpose?
These are perennial questions
which any reflection about life
inevitably brings to mind.
Lord, such questions are in my mind,
not because I feel my life lacks purpose.
My faith and the variety of experiences
in the past and the present
have filled my life with meaning and purpose -
and I give you my heartfelt thanks.
It is the deep sense of wonder
which makes such questions persist.
Lord, sometimes, on a clear night
when the moon is shining and all is calm,
I find myself gazing into the star-spangled sky
and I share the Psalmist's feeling of awe and wonder
which brought from him the response –
" When I look at the sky,
which you have made,
at the moon and the stars,
which you set in their places -
what are human beings, that you think of them;
mere mortals, that you care for them?"

I suspect, Lord,
that you will not be giving me answers

which remove the mystery!
Perhaps it is the element of mystery -
the unknowing,
the gradual unfolding of the future, which,
though often disturbing,
fills life with its true meaning, and
encourages me to reach out after you.

My child, never lose that deep sense of wonder:
hold on to that feeling of awe
as you reflect on life with all its variety of experiences.
Persist with your questions:
it is the element of unknowing
which keeps you reaching out to me.

There is an answer to your question,
"who am I?"
You are an individual, a unique person –
there is only one of you!
What is more, you bear my image -
you have kinship with me -
you have the potential to follow
desires like mine- the capacity to love
and to respond to love.
I am sure that does not dispel all the mystery -
nor would I wish it to!
Indeed you are right –

it is the unknowing
which makes your life
the great adventure which it is.
It is the mystery which keeps you
reaching out through the mists of unknowing,
and always, I am there with you.

Lord, help me to be still..

"Be still and know that I am God",
Lord, these words from Psalm 46
keep coming to mind.
Perhaps, you are trying to tell me something!
In other, more modern translations of the Psalm
I find the same thought expressed in different ways-
"Calm down, and learn that I am God" -
"Stop fighting and know that I am God" -
"Let go of your concerns,
then you will know that I am God" -
"Step out of the traffic!
Take a long, loving look at me, your High God".
Interesting variations -
all of them directing me towards you!
This is, of course, about prayer, isn't it?
I do know that prayer is much more than
using the right words and phrases;
I do appreciate that it is essentially
about being still, letting go of my worries for a time,
and in that stillness,
appreciating your presence -
knowing that you are God.
It is giving you the chance to talk to me

in the quietness of my mind.
Lord, I am grateful for the times
when that has been my experience.
But "stepping out of the traffic",
"calming down", "stopping fighting", "being still" -
isn't all that easy!
There are so many other distractions
in the midst of a busy, often noisy world
which tend to push thoughts of you
to the back of my mind.
Maybe, Lord, I am too busy trying to serve you,
that I neglect spending time, quietly with you.
Lord, forgive me – I am making lame excuses -
in fact, I am not even being
totally honest with myself – or with you!
When I say I am busy serving you,
perhaps I am really busy serving myself
and my own interests -
busy with activities which please me,
while telling myself that in them, I am serving you!
Lord, help me to be still more often:
and in the stillness, not only
to take a long, hard look at myself but also
to take a long, loving look at you:
to know that truly, you are my Lord and my God.

My child, of course I am trying
to tell you something!
Do you think that your relationship with me
is just about what you do for me -
going to worship -
playing some part in the life of the Church,
trying to be of service to others?
All of which, of course, pleases me.
But you know very well that
a relationship with me goes way beyond that.
Sitting quietly with me –
allowing yourself to be aware of my presence,
in spite of the mystery -
even amid the noise and clamour of everyday life,
feeling a sense of awe and wonder.
Your efforts at serving me will then be enriched -
enabling you from the stillness,
to become, more effectively for others,
an instrument of my peace.

Lord, in green pastures or dark valleys, be my Shepherd...

Lord, as the words of that
well-loved Psalm come to mind,
I appreciate again, how relevant
the insights of the Psalmist are
in our busy, rushing modern world,
just as much as they were to him.
The more I reflect on these words,
the more I realise what
a staggering expression of faith in you,
this really is!
We often associate this Psalm with a funeral service,
with the comforting words
about your presence in the dark valley
to which, of course, they are so appropriate,
but we should never lose sight
of how relevant the faith expressed in this psalm
is to our everyday lives.

Perhaps David was the author and
I imagine him quietly reflecting on his life -
casting his mind back to his youth as a shepherd,
before the burden of kingship was thrust upon him:
remembering the peaceful,

idyllic days in the green pastures
beside the quiet, fresh flowing waters of the stream.
Was he perhaps giving thanks to you
for such peaceful days which he still experienced,
in spite of the pressures of ruling his people?
Was he seeking reassurance from these memories,
because he was aware that the path ahead,
almost certainly would lead through a dark valley?

Lord, as I look back over my life,
I give you thanks for the countless times
when you have certainly led me by still waters
and into green pastures:
you have been with me,
even when I have forgotten you,
enriching and giving meaning to my life.
I have also faced many dark valleys -
some of them more threatening than others,
but always you have been there
with your reassuring presence,
reviving my flagging spirit and
restoring my trust in you.
There have been times when
I have strayed from the path
you would have me follow.
But with your forgiving love,
you have called me back,
to what the Psalmist has called,
"the paths of righteousness",
just as the shepherd has urged his flock
to follow where he leads, for

he knows it is the way of safety.
The Psalmist, it appears, is aware that
these "paths of righteousness"
lead him into a closer relationship with you,
and he feels that, in spite of his failings,
you treat him like an honoured guest –
spreading a table before him and
anointing his head with oil.
Lord, help me to maintain
such a relationship with you and
always to be aware of your presence,
not only in the darkest of the valleys
through which I may have to pass,
but each day as it comes.

My child, these words,
certainly are relevant to your life,
even though they come to you
from an age, long past, and
from a life style, so different
to that of the modern world.
I remain, to those who trust me,
the unchanging Lord,
the loving shepherd, the wise guide,
the forgiving companion of the soul –
enabling those who trust me,
to face bravely, the reality of life,
however challenging it may be.
Of course you have treasured
my comforting presence in
the dark valley of bereavement.

But you have also known my presence
and my guiding support in the many times
when you have been led through the green pastures
and beside the still waters!
Be assured - My goodness and mercy will be with you,
all the days of your life.

Lord, what is true joy...?

Lord, recently in my city,
on boards enclosing empty shops,
there was an invitation to passers-by
to write a comment in response to
the statement, "Before I die...."
There have been some very strange wishes –
some of them, in fact, being very moving,
leaving me wondering
what has been going on in the life of the writer.
Not surprisingly, many wanted to become rich!
But the majority indicated a wish to be happy.
I feel sure that is a desire of which you would approve!

But, what is the nature of true happiness?
Jesus on many occasions talked about joy.
He told His friends, even as He tried
to make them aware of the fate which awaited Him, -
"These things I have spoken to you
that my joy may be in you
and that your joy may be full."
That brings to mind that wonderful hymn,
"O love, that will not let me go", with the verse,
"O joy that seeks for me through pain,
I cannot close my heart to Thee;

I trace the rainbow through the rain
and feel the promise is not vain,
that morn shall tearless be."

The hymn writer appears to be expressing the belief
that the true joy which can enrich our lives,
is one which comes through
the humiliation and pain of the Cross
which you endured in Jesus?
I find his words as a poignant reminder
that I ought to rejoice about the cross,
for through such pain and suffering,
you were giving expression
to your amazing and undeserved love –
a love which you assure us, will never let us go.
But Lord, this joy is often missing in my life!
I allow so many adverse circumstances
to dampen my spirit and to fan the flames of discontent -
and yet I know how truly fortunate I am,
surrounded by your love.
Lord, forgive me for the many times
when I look elsewhere
for my flagging spirit to be revived.
Can I really know this true joy,
in spite of the dark days I still experience?

My child, remember, such true joy
is not an over-exuberant, bubbly affair:
It is rather a quiet confidence,
an inner peace, a calming contentment -
and, as the hymn writer is also implying,
it is a joy which can be known,
even in the midst of pain, enabling you to
"trace the rainbow through the rain"!
Bear in mind how my joy was still with you,
in the loss of your loved one:
it is with you even in the darkest of days,
which you still experience .
As you already know,
the life of faith is not an escape route
which avoids the ills and set backs of life;
faith does not transform life into a soft option!
But even through the pain,
there can still be the deep seated joy –
the contentment
which comes from knowing that
you will never be alone.
Even in the midst of sadness,
joy still visits you; it comes in a variety of ways -
often unexpected -
the memories of experiences
shared with your beloved:

the smile which so often, brightened your day:
the first signs of spring as
the harshness of winter fades:
witnessing an act of loving compassion:
seeing the blossoming of love
between two who are dear to you:
hearing the strains of wonderful, inspiring music -
so many ways in which joy
interrupts the saddest of days.
Treasure these moments and
recognise my presence with you in them all.

Lord, I'm sorry but I do worry...

Lord, how often I have said, to other folk
addressing a wide variety of situations,
"Don't worry!"
even though I know in my heart
that worry, anxiety, is an inevitable part of life.
I remember as a young minister,
preaching a sermon to which I gave the title
"Don't Worry"!
I recall suggesting that, as Christians,
we should not worry because
we have put our trust in you:
we should take seriously what Jesus
said to His disciples on a number of occasions,
telling them not to worry.
We should take to heart the words of Paul
in his letter to the Phillipian Church -
" Don't worry about anything, but
in all your prayers ask God for what you need".

Experience has taught me to review
the way I regard such words:
anxiety will always be part of living –

and also a part of loving!
I dare to suggest that Jesus also faced times of worry.
Was He not facing worry in the lonely days
we call "The Temptations?
Is not His anxiety reflected in
His agonised prayer in Gethsemane,
"Father, if it be possible, let this cup pass from me" -
an intense and most understandable human worry?

Lord, I want to be totally honest and realistic
about anxieties which crop up in my life.
Sometimes they may be about health,
maybe about mistakes I know I have made,
perhaps about the future –
speculating about "what if..." situations:
or concern about the future of the Church -
Of course it helps when I talk to you
about such worries, but they are still there!

My child, of course you are right!
Facing anxieties is all part of being human.
Of course, even Jesus faced worrying situations:
if He didn't, He would not have been truly human.
Many of your worries are because you love!
To love, to care is to expose yourself
to anxiety.
If those you love are facing trouble,

how worthless would your love be if you did not care?
Reflect on this also –
worry is often you trying
to find a solution to the problem,
so don't feel guilty about it!
Share it with me:
always, I am your Lord who cares.
The problem will not always go away,
but together, we can cope!
Let your mind be sharpened
as you grapple with all that life can throw at you,
for there is nothing in the whole of creation
which can separate you from my love.
I am Lord of the present and of the future -
I am the companion who walks with you,
however troublesome the road
may sometimes appear be.

Lord, did you make a mistake...?

Lord, I have been thinking about
Simon, the fisherman, whom you called
to be one of your disciples:
you renamed him Peter, "the rock".
There appears to have been no hesitation
in his response to your invitation –
immediately, he was up for the challenge!
Later on, you even said to him,
"on this rock I will build my church!"
In the light of later events,
you must often have wondered,
"have I made a terrible mistake?
Is he really up to the challenge,
not only of being one of my men,
but also the added responsibility
I am putting on him?"

You even called him "Satan"
when he told you not to talk such rubbish,
when you tried to warn him of the fate
which you knew lay ahead!
You told him that he was not on your side

but on the side of men!
It was the same Peter who, in these moments of
vision at what we call "The Tranfiguration,"
prattled on in the most embarrassing way,
only to be told that he should be listening to you. -
The same arrogant Peter
who attempted to walk with you
on the stormy waters of Galilee
only to sink because his faith failed him.
This is the man who,
at the time of your arrest in Gethsemane,
thought he should try to defend you with a weapon,
only hours later, vehemently to deny
that he had anything to do with you!
What an incredibly shaky foundation
on which to establish your Church!

But Lord, I am so glad you did!
Every time I read about Peter,
I see something of myself!
Often, I too, in the face of matters of the spirit,
don't know what to say
and embarrass myself
by blurting out the wrong words:
I too, feel myself sinking
when I try, bravely, to face the storms alone
and my faith fails me!

I, too, find it all too easy,
to remain quiet about my relationship with you.
Is my loyalty to you, really any different from Peter's?
Yet, just as you chose Peter,
you have also called me!
In spite of my weaknesses, my failures -
you still want me to be with you –
to serve you – to represent you in the world of today.
How unworthy I am!

My child, there was no mistake!
How off-putting to others would it have been,
if I was surrounded by perfect followers -
folk who never made any mistakes?
The rock on which the Church is built
and on which it still stands is one of
doubt, weakness and failure -
but in spite of that –
or should I say, because of that,
my kingdom still conquers
the hearts and minds of those
prepared to respond with love
when confronted by my challenge.
Remember how I, the risen Lord,
confronted Peter and his companions
by the lake side:
they didn't even recognise me!

I challenged Peter with the question,
"Peter, do you love me?"
Peter, in his usual impulsive way,
responded, "You know that I do!"
I persisted by asking the question twice more,
and could see the same impatience
as Peter vehemently emphasised his
undying love for me.
And, of course, I knew he meant it!
I also knew there would still be mistakes,
there would still be failures,
but I knew that my love for him - and for you:
and his genuine response –
and yours - of love for me,
imperfect though it may be,
is the true foundation for my kingdom.

Lord, I want to be part of your kingdom...

Lord, I reflect on the words from John's Gospel,
"Except a man be born again,
he cannot see the kingdom of God" -
and I affirm that I do want to be part of your kingdom
I also remember that you said
"whoever does not receive the Kingdom of God
like a child will never enter it".
Were you then giving expression
to the same idea as being "born again"?
I suppose I like to regard myself as 'mature',
both as a person and as a Christian -
but, on reflection, I would be happy to be known
as a 'childlike Christian',
Perhaps you are looking for me to display
in my relationship with you,
more of the wonderful childlike qualities, such as
wide-eyed wonder as I try
to absorb the greatness of your love:
the quality of childlike innocence,
the lack of prejudice or suspicion,
a child's ability to live for the moment,
not afraid of the future,

eager to take new steps in company with you:
an eagerness to be loved
and the ability to respond, without reservation,
to love which is shown:
especially a childlike trust to face the mystery of life,
displaying curiosity and-
a willingness to explore with you,
new avenues of experience
as layer after layer of reality and of love unfolds,
enriching life with a reassuring
awareness of your presence -
inspiring a confidence that
I really am part of your Kingdom.

Perhaps I need to be 'reborn'
to my faith each day if I am to possess
these childlike qualities
in a meaningful and practical way -
making a new start and-
renewing my relationship with you -
realising anew, the wonder of your love.

My child, being "born again" or
"becoming like a child" is not
a once for all experience!
Begin each new day as it comes with me.
Paul, in his letter to the Colossians,

wrote about the need to stand firm
as mature and fully convinced Christians.
Growing to maturity is a life-long process!
Never lose that wide-eyed wonder –
that feeling of awe as you reflect on
and appreciate my love.
Never lose the eagerness to move forward in your faith:
continue to learn new aspects of my love;
become aware of the many ways in
which my presence is with you, and
the challenges I invite you to face.
You most certainly are a part of my Kingdom -
a part of the great multitude, worldwide,
who have responded to the appeal of my love.

Campbell Miller

Lord, it isn't always easy to hope...

Lord, we often talk about "Christian hope" and
I know that the Christian Gospel is
essentially a message which is full of hope
but I am very conscious of often
using the word "hopeless"
about all sorts of situations -
problems in society –
disturbing conflicts around the world
and the resulting desperate human suffering.
I often find myself wondering if even our prayers
about such distressing issues
will ever make any difference!

Yet, I am reminded that such pessimism
is in sharp contrast to the hope displayed
by many of the men and women of the Bible,
and indeed, by many of the great Christian souls
of countless generations right up to today –
and I feel ashamed!
What is it that inspires such hope?
I suppose it must be an enduring faith
in your almighty power and goodness:

perhaps also, faith in the potential
for goodness in humankind,
in spite of the evil and tragic events
which so often dominate the news?

But Lord, it isn't easy to hold on to such hope!
And yet – I do regard myself as an optimistic person!
Recently, I found that optimism
being challenged especially by the view that
"optimism is the belief that things will get better-
hope is the belief that, if we work hard enough,
we can make things better!."
I suppose optimism does not take much courage –
it is often a case of saying to oneself –
"it will all work out in the end – don't worry about it!"
I admit that reflects a very naïve view.
I do need your help to a clearer understanding
about faith and hope.
My faith in you does suggest to me that
there should be nothing
which really deserves to be labelled "hopeless",
but Lord, I still find it impossible
not to recognise that there are so many,
both in my community and around the world,
for whom hope has long since
moved well out of their grasp -
they are deprived of everything

which makes life worth-while and meaningful,
indeed, makes life possible at all.
Lord, help me, I pray, for I do want
to look out on life with hope and with faith,
but often find it difficult.

**My child, I do understand.
I cannot give you all the answers,
for my gift of human freedom means
that people do not always act
in the way that I would wish!
Continue to reflect on what you said to me that
"hope is the belief that, if we work hard enough,
we can make things better!"
Faith in me alone does not magically
bring hope to your "hopeless" situations -
it is human effort which does that!
Think of the New Testament words
in the Letter of James:**

*"what good is it for one of you to say that you have faith
if your actions do not prove it?...
Suppose there are brothers or sisters
who need clothes and don't have enough to eat.
What good is there in your saying to them,
"God bless you! Keep warm and eat well!"--
if you don't give them the necessities of life?*

So it is with faith:
if it is alone and includes no actions, then it is dead."

Faith in me is not a matter of naive optimism
which sees life as you would like it to be -
or believing that mere wishing or praying
will make it so
True faith in me opens your eyes
to see life exactly as it is,
but also enables you to see that
even in the valley of the shadow,
there are always glimmerings of light ahead.
And in relation to your so-called "hopeless" situations,
it is your human efforts which
will contribute to these flickering lights of hope,
however weak they sometimes appear to be.
In the midst of all the complexities
of life as you experience it,
remain assured that I,
the Lord of the Kingdom of Hope
will always be with you.

Campbell Miller

Lord, on days when I feel alone...

Lord, there are times when I do feel lonely:
I am sure it is a common experience.
It is not just when sitting at home,
with only the voices on television or radio for company –
it can also be when surrounded by many people -
but I don't know any of them!

Such loneliness, of course, can be good -
but not too much of it!
It does make me reflect, without any distractions,
on a wide variety of issues -
especially on my faith
and, perhaps, it is then that I am
more aware of you speaking to me.
Often in these lonely moments,
you seem to be breaking in to
the turmoil of confused and distressing thoughts
with your calming influence
and the quiet reassurance of your presence.
I have no doubt that these
conversations which we have,
often develop through such moments of loneliness

when you remind me that I am never alone.
But, Lord, while I appreciate
the awareness of your presence,
often the loneliness remains –
there is still the craving for human company:
talking with you is great,
but so is human conversation.
Looking back over years of ministry,
perhaps, too often,
the comfort I have offered to lonely folk has been
to reassure them that **you** are with them,
when the great need was for
the warmth and support of human contact -
the healing, reassuring quality of friendship,
so perhaps I failed them.

Lord, in these moments of loneliness,
I do feel guilty, when the fact that
you are always there has been
pushed to the back of my mind:
and then I remember that–
there is nothing which can separate me from your love,
and that is truly wonderful –
but I hope you will forgive me when I say -
if loneliness is to be banished,
I still need people!

My child, of course you do!
An awareness of my presence with you
is certainly something you should treasure -
you matter to me.
But always remember -
life is essentially about relationships.
The writers of the ancient Genesis stories of Creation,
certainly reflected very well my divine will
when they said, "It is not good for man to be alone"!
Let your times of loneliness
remind you that others are lonely too!
You are feeling a need of them –
but they too, need you!

Lord, I often worry about the way we use the Lord's Prayer'...

Our Father, who art in Heaven,
hallowed be thy name,
thy kingdom come;
thy will be done on earth as it is in heaven.
Give us this day our daily bread.
And forgive us our trespasses,
as we forgive those who trespass against us.
And lead us not into temptation,
but deliver us from evil.
For thine is the kingdom, the power, and the glory,
for ever and ever.
Amen.

Lord, these words are so familiar!
I, and countless others,
repeat them so often,
and I must confess, hardly think of them as a prayer,
let alone reflecting
on the meaning of what I am saying!
We know them as "the Lord's Prayer"
for, according to the Gospels,
this was Jesus' response to a request
from His disciples,
"Lord, teach us how to pray".
Maybe, these are the exact words of His response –
or maybe it is a prayer
put together by His followers,
encompassing many aspects of His teaching -
either way, it does not matter, for
I see this as "The Lord's Prayer" –
words which I should not be
repeating casually or without meaning,
but reverently and with understanding.

As, quietly, I reflect on these very special words
I begin to appreciate
how challenging a prayer it is
and wonder how I have dared to treat it so casually!

My child, it is indeed, a very special prayer -
but every prayer, when offered to me
with sincerity, is special
and brings spiritual renewal and strength
to those who come with the desire
to know me and to love me.
Do reflect carefully on the challenges
which these words hold out to you.
Always remember that prayer is not
just you talking to me,
but an opportunity for me
to communicate with you, and to challenge you.

1." Our Father, who art in Heaven, hallowed be thy name".

Lord, how can I dare to use
casually or thoughtlessly these words
which are intended
as an expression of worship?
I should be challenging myself to reverence you -
I should be standing in awe of your greatness,
your majesty, your almighty power.
I should be lost in wonder,
as I am reminded of the crowning aspect
of your magnificent being - your Fatherly love
and your concern for your creation.
Though I use the words, "who art in Heaven",
I rejoice in the glorious mystery that
you are not confined to some state we call Heaven,
but I can know you as the Lord,
present with me:
one with whom I can share my deepest thoughts.

When I pray "Hallowed be thy name",
I ought to be quietly reflecting on what that means.
Since, in line with Biblical thought, "name"
means far more than the label
by which someone is called -
this surely refers to your personality, your very being, -
to everything about you –
So right from the start of this prayer,
my spirit should be bowing before you to honour you,

the almighty, eternal, loving Father God,
much of whose being is enshrouded in mystery
and yet has made Himself known to us in Jesus.

**My child, the challenge which confronts you
as you pray these words, certainly is
to focus your attention on me:
to encourage the spiritual side of your nature
to reach out to me in sincere worship.
However, bound up with that,
is the other challenge -
to give to me, not merely worship,
but loving service.
You honour me by serving me:
you honour me by facing up to
the other challenges which will confront you
as, with sincerity and faith,
you pray the rest of this prayer.**

2. "...Thy kingdom come..."

Lord, for what am I really praying
with these words?
Other versions of the Gospels express
this in different ways:
one says, "come and set up your kingdom",
another, "Let your kingdom come",
and yet another does not mention "kingdom",
but simply says, "set the world to right"!
These don't help me!

So I look at other words of Jesus about "the Kingdom" -
especially the parables
which He often introduced with the words,
"the kingdom of God is like..."
and I believe that by "the kingdom", He was meaning,
"the rule of God in the lives of people" -
you ruling as King in our lives.
So Lord, when I pray this prayer,
perhaps I should be thinking of these words
as my invitation to you to rule as King in my life!
I am afraid that, too often when uttering these words,
I have been expressing a wish
for your Kingdom to grow -
for your rule to encompass our world,
without thinking of the challenge to me.

Lord, forgive me and help me to face
the challenge of this prayer:
that I may play my part, however small,
in making your Kingdom come.

Yes, my child, it is all too easy to pray mere words.
You really want my kingdom to grow?
You really want my rule to be more widely recognised?
Then, your prayer must come from the heart!
The challenge to you is to remember each day --
I, the Lord, do want to rule in your life!

3. "...Thy will be done on earth as it is in Heaven..."

Lord, how often I have used these words
and have not thought of all the implications!
All too often it is what I want
that is important to me!
Here am I praying for your will to be done!
What am I thinking when I repeat this in Church –
or indeed, at any time
when using the words of the Lord's Prayer?
I am afraid that, more often than not,
(if, indeed, I am paying attention to the words!),
I am expressing my wish
for your will to be done on earth, in general,
in international affairs, in public life,
in decisions which affect our lives in society.
I am hoping that your will, will prevail
throughout the life of the world.
I find it very easy to pray for all that –
it makes no great demands on me!
I even feel a sense of pride
for having prayed such a prayer!
But what about my life?
What about your will being done in my life?
Lord, help me to reflect on this challenge,

I am reminded of how grateful I should be
for your wondrous gift of free will!
I am not like some puppet,
made to dance at the whim of you,
the Divine puppet master!
I am free to make choices -
but I know that all too often
I do not choose as I should.
Lord, help me to resolve this conflict
between what I want and what you want,
and what you expect, from me.
And when I pray "your will be done",
help me to mean what I say.

My child, even Jesus faced this conflict:
you remember His prayer to me at Gethsemane,
as the cross seemed to loom high on His horizon:
"Father, if it be possible, let this cup pass from me";
then His faith, and His courage, triumphed -
He prayed again,
"Father, not my will, but yours!"
Can you imagine the upsurge of love
in my Divine Being at this response?
By all means, express the hope
for my will to be done throughout the world -
but always remember,   you have your part to play -
your peace to be found in seeking – and doing my will..

4." ...give us this day, our daily bread..."

Lord, I don't think I have ever thought
seriously about these words as I have prayed this prayer!
This is probably the part which I allow
most easily to roll off my tongue in a careless fashion!
I am not helped by some slight variations in a few
other versions of the Gospels -
one says, "give us our food for today":
another has "give us today, the food we need",
while a third expresses it, in my view,
rather outrageously, with the words,
"keep us alive with three square meals"!

Would I calmly pray this, were I living
in a place devastated by famine, drought,
flooding, or any other natural disaster:
a situation where my childrens' bellies
are swollen from lack of sustenance, and
I also am facing a lingering death?
My prayer, if I prayed at all, might be for
one of the relief agencies to arrive,
before it is too late!
Lord, forgive me for my selfish ingratitude
as I take for granted my comfortable life,
compared to that of countless others.
Forgive me when I am tempted to regard

these words as a pointless part of the prayer
Inspire me, instead with thoughts of gratitude:
challenge to show greater concern
for those who do not know what it is like
to have 'daily bread'.

My child, you do not need forgiveness
for thinking like that – indeed it
would be more appropriate to seek forgiveness
if you continue to use these words in a
careless and meaningless way!
But use them you should!
Don't regard it as a petition -
a request addressed to me,
but rather as a meditation –
a stimulus to other thoughts and reflections.
It should inspire gratitude for the
degree of good fortune which is yours.
Thoughts about those less fortunate
should come flooding into your mind with these words.
That especially is what makes this
such a challenging part of the whole prayer -
it should be leading you to ask yourself,
from your comfortable situation of plenty –
"what am I doing to change the fortunes of others?"

5. "... **forgive us our trespasses, as we forgive those who trespass against us..."**

Lord, this is certainly a part of the prayer
which I do know I ought to take seriously!
I am very aware of the challenge here!
I do need to ask for your forgiveness,
for I know only too well,
how far short I fall of the standard
you expect from me.
I know also, that I am not very good
at showing forgiveness to others.
I am afraid that, when I repeat this prayer,
especially if it is along with the rest of the congregation,
usually, my own failures are
easily banished to the back of my mind, and
I find myself thinking of our collective failures -
failures of the Church,
failures within our local community,
failures in society -
anything but those failures in myself –
issues which damage my relationship with you.
Lord, remind me again and again of
the challenge of these words.
Help me to avoid whatever

spoils my relationship with you -
Help me, especially, to understand that
any grievance I hold against someone else -
any broken relationship which I refuse to heal,
damages my relationship with you -
a relationship which I treasure,
but which, all too often I spoil
by my selfish pursuit of my own wishes.
Lord, forgive me – and help me
to forgive others, as readily as you are to forgive me.

My child, forgiveness can be hard:
broken relationships are hurtful.
It is not easy to forget the hurt
the pleasure of retaliation.
It is not easy to say "sorry" –
it is especially hurtful to pride!
But never lose sight
of the cost of my forgiveness.
To convince you of my love -
to challenge you to turn from your selfishness -
to bring the healing and wholeness
of forgiveness to humankind -
it all involved the suffering
of Him, who even in the midst of it,
could pray "Father, forgive them,
they don't know what they are doing!"

6. "...Lead us not into temptation, and deliver us from evil"

Lord, do you really tempt us?
Do you really lead us into difficult situations,
tempting us to give up our faith?
Of course you don't!
That surely would not be the action of
a loving, Heavenly Father!
But temptation is certainly something
I do experience and I know
that I don't always resist when I should.
Is it that there is an evil tendency in me
which tempts me to follow
my own selfish desires, rather than
doing what I know to be right?
I wonder what I am actually asking
when I pray this prayer.
Surely it should be for the help of your
loving presence when I am tempted.
I do recognise that
need to be protected from
whatever evil tendencies there are in me.
I do need also to be delivered from
whatever evil influences may confront me in
life as they sometimes do.
Grant to me the strength and the courage to resist
and uphold me by the power of your love.

My child, our earlier conversation
about my will being done, touched on this.
As you said then, I am no divine puppet master
pulling the strings, forcing you to go
the way I would like you to go.
Temptation is the price of such freedom!
Being human means
that you are always facing choices.
Perhaps the best light is shed on
the nature of temptation by reflecting on
what the Gospels tell you
about Jesus being tempted,
for He was no stranger to temptation.
There He was, just having experienced
moments of vision as He was baptised by John,
hearing my voice which confirmed for Him,
who He really was – my Son, my chosen One.
Now He had to face the question of
what path He must follow to do my will.
So in a lonely place, He thought and He prayed:
various, tempting ways forward occurred to Him,
but after many days, He committed Himself
to the path which inevitably, would lead to the cross.
Again, in Gethsemane,
He was aware of temptation when,
in His agony of spirit, He was asking me
to take this cup of suffering away from Him -

but then, He gained the courage
and the strength from me
to turn away from such temptation.

I do not lead you into temptation -
my child, it is life –
it is being human which does that!
But reach out to me – just as Jesus did:
my strengthening presence
is always there for you also.
I will indeed uphold you with the power of my love.

7..." For thine is the kingdom, the power, and the glory, for ever and ever. Amen."

Lord, how appropriate that this special prayer
ends, as it began, with an expression of worship!
But it is even more than that!
It is a declaration of faith,
it is a celebration,
a recognition that, however much
your eternal being is enshrouded in mystery,
it is a glorious mystery and through it,
you confront me -
you challenge me -
you reassure me.
I will still face temptations -
evil influences may still surround me:
I will still need, confession, repentance
and your forgiveness, for failures may still be mine.
But, yours is the Kingdom into which you have called me –
always the power is yours
and you offer that power to me,
to live and work for your glory –
for the glory of your Kingdom
which is for ever and ever!

My child, I urge you,
continue to pray the words of this prayer with meaning.

You have rightly called this
"a challenging prayer",   which it most surely is.
Continue to resist the temptation
to let any of these words roll off your tongue
casually and thoughtlessly:
do not treat them as empty meaningless phrases
from an age long past.
Continue to reflect on them,
relate them to each new day as you pray.
It is truly, a challenging prayer, and
as you pray these words,
today's challenge to you,
may not be same as that of yesterday,
or as that of tomorrow -
for always the demands of living
as part of my Kingdom
will be relevant to each new day.
My Kingdom is for ever and ever – and
I need you as part of it!

Lord, Creeds worry me...

Lord, for many years I have regarded myself as a Christian –
sometimes, I am sure, not a very good one!
Am I less of a Christian
if I find it difficult, if not impossible,
to subscribe to certain beliefs -
beliefs which may, for example,
be summarised in a creed?
My knowledge of Church history tells me that
beliefs have been held to be so important
by so many over the centuries that,
thousands, if not millions have been tortured,
imprisoned, or even killed
because they held beliefs contrary
to what was regarded as the official "correct" dogma!
Religious history is littered with stories
of so many so-called "heretics",
most of whom now, in fact, would be seen as shining
examples of true faith!
It is all very confusing!
Lord, surely, you cannot have wanted all this to happen?

Now, among Christians, we do not usually find such
extreme actions over differences in belief,
but there is still a great deal of intolerance -
I, also have to admit that there are times when
I am not as tolerant of those
who disagree with me as I should be!

Lord, all this makes me somewhat suspicious of creeds!
Surely it is sad that the movement begun by Jesus,
which was essentially about love,
has developed over the centuries to a system
of dogma which are supposed to be believed
if one is to be regarded as a true Christian.

If I am ever in a Church service in which
we are invited to recite the words of a creed,
I am conscious of asking myself –
do I really believe that? – and
if I am not sure that I do, does that offend you?
Am I any less a Christian if I cannot honestly
subscribe to some of these dogmatic statements?

My child, of course the martyrdom
of so many Christian souls in past generations
grieved me deeply. How could it be otherwise?
Love is of such supreme importance
and must be at the heart of being truly my disciple.
And I am still grieved by the bitter disputes over doctrine
– or even the correct way to offer worship
which, sadly, divides those who share faith in me.
Of course not everyone
wants to offer worship to me in exactly the same way.
There are so many different ways
in which sincere worship may be expressed:
sincerity and true devotion is what is important.
Do you remember the conversation
Jesus had with that Samaritan woman?

There were bitter disagreements between
Jews and Samaritans – even disagreeing about where
valid worship could take place!
As if that was important!
Of course it is acceptable to worship me
with sincerity anywhere, and
in whatever way allows you to feel near to me.
No, of course, I am not offended
by your problem with some
of the dogmatic statements in a creed –
that shows that you take your faith seriously;
honest reflection is much more important
than blind, unthinking acceptance.

However, a creed can be a useful basis
for reflection about the faith
so long as the validity of faith
is not judged by acceptance
or rejection of parts of the creed.
Let me assure you, my criteria for judgement
has nothing to do with the dogma you hold – or reject.
Remember how Jesus told
the Parable of the Sheep and the Goats -
There is no mention of holding right beliefs –
the only criteria is – "how much did you care?"
Did you serve me by the care and service
you gave to other people?
Take these statements of the creed -
reflect quietly and honestly on them:
if you question some of them

talk to me about them –
I am confident that together,
we will draw out from them,
thoughts which relate to your daily living
and your relationship with me
as you pursue your pilgrimage of faith.

Lord, can I talk to you about the Apostles' Creed...

*I believe in God, the Father almighty,
creator of Heaven and earth.
I believe in Jesus Christ, God's only Son, our
Lord, who was conceived by the Holy Spirit,
born of the Virgin Mary, suffered under
Pontius Pilate, was crucified, died and was
buried. He descended into hell. On the
third day He rose again.
He ascended into heaven, He is seated at
the right hand of the Father and He will
come to judge the living and the dead.
I believe in the Holy Spirit, the Holy
Catholic Church, the communion of saints,
the forgiveness of sins, the resurrection of
the body, and the life everlasting.*

1. I believe in God, the Father almighty, creator of Heaven and earth.

Lord, of course I believe in you –
otherwise, I wouldn't be talking to you like this!
I cannot prove that you exist –
I cannot see you: I cannot penetrate,
as much as I would like,
the mystery of your eternal Being - but,
in the face of all that suggests otherwise,
I affirm my belief that you are the Creator.
Despite all the other views
which suggest that creation just happened,
I cling to my conviction that behind
all the wonder of the world and the universe,
your creating power was at work.
I look at the wonderful stories in Genesis:
while I cannot accept them
as factual accounts of creation,
I see them as reflecting profound human insights
which convey a deeply held truth,
introduced with the most significant words -
"in the beginning, God..."
Whatever science may tell us, I hold fast to that
and I honour you and worship you as Creator God,
the Source and Sustainer of all life.

But I also honour and worship you as Father.
You are our Father God, our beginning and our ending -
the source of all our lives and

I give you my grateful thanks.
Seeing you as Father,
reminds me of your dominating attribute – Love!
Lord, when I declare that I believe in you,
I am conscious that I should be embracing more fully,
the Father's love you offer to me –
forgive me, I pray:
help me more readily to come to you,
as I would to an earthly Father,
seeking advice, accepting offers of help,
listening to what you say to me
in the many ways in which you communicate.
Above all, help me to respond to your love.

My child, I am glad you can declare your belief
that, though you cannot see me,
you recognise me as the source of your life-
Especially I rejoice that you own me
as Father God –
that you want to embrace more fully
the love I have for you.
Continue to respond to my love -
"belief" always must be more than
intellectual acceptance by the mind:
true belief is action –
true belief is trust -
true belief is commitment.

Lord, I do believe –
please help me where my faith falls short.

2. "I believe in Jesus Christ, God's only Son, our Lord, who was conceived by the Holy Spirit, born of the Virgin Mary..."

Lord, of course I believe in Jesus:
I want to be known as one of His people and,
because I put my trust in Him,
somehow , in my spirit I know His presence with me
in a way which I don't really understand
and which I can't really put into words.

I am not sure I understand all the theology
involved in talking about Him as "your only son"!
Of course, He was special – you sent Him!
More than that, although it is a great mystery
beyond my understanding,
I believe that He was, in fact,
you, come to live among us,
to share the reality of human life,
and I treasure that.

But, Lord, I hope you will forgive me –
"Born of the Virgin Mary" does raise
a question in my mind.
If I accept this literally, then it means that
Jesus' life didn't really begin
like mine with a human father.

I am aware that this is one of the issues
which divides Christians –
for some, belief in this Virgin Birth
is of the utmost importance –
and I respect their view.
But for others of us, the special nature of Jesus
does not rest on that, but
on your divine spirit infilling Him
and being embodied in Him.
So Lord, I dare to say, I don't think it matters,
and if I am wrong, I stand judged by you!

But Lord, I still find in this a great deal for reflection.
Mary must have been a very special person
to be chosen by you to give birth to Jesus:
It also makes me think that, even leaving aside
the question of the Virgin birth,
Joseph, too, must have been a very special person,
to be entrusted with
the care and nurture of this very special child!

This part of the creed, leads me to reflect
on the thought that, with great humility,
Mary carried the holy presence of Jesus
in her body for nine whole months –
then, she nurtured Him as a baby,
as a growing child, as a teenager,

continuing to love Him as a young man,
playing her part in shaping His character,
challenging his mistakes,
(for if He was truly human, He must have made them.).
She had the heart-rending experience
of seeing her son cruelly put to death on the cross.

Lord, as I reflect on these words from the creed,
direct me away from the controversial thoughts –
instead, remind me that, I too,
like Mary, though in a different way,
have the privilege, but also the responsibility
for carrying His presence, -
which also means, your presence, -
to the world around me.

Lord, help me to shoulder that responsibility
more faithfully, and give me
the strength and the courage
to carry with me, day by day,
the joy and wonder of your presence.

**My child, there is no need to apologise
for your questioning what after all, are
only theological attempts to probe the mystery.
What is important is holding on to
your faith and your relationship with me.
Put to one side, the theological terminology,**

which sadly, can divide my people:
concentrate rather on fostering
that precious relationship with Jesus,
who, in response to faith, however weak,
transforms your life and fills it with meaning.

3. "...suffered under Pontius Pilate, was crucified, died and was buried."

Lord, this is part of the creed
about which there can be no controversy!
It states a historical fact which can hardly be disputed.
But, of course, I am far from comfortable
with the fact of the suffering Jesus –
a suffering which is so much more
than just the awful, physical suffering
of death on the cross:
it was also the agony of being misunderstood -
the rejection by those He came to serve.
I too must stand guilty of misunderstanding
and sometimes rejecting
the love which He freely offers me.

Lord, as I reflect on these words from the Creed,
help me also to appreciate that there is here,
so much more than a statement of fact
about the death of Jesus on the cross.
Help me to remember that you are God
who shares the suffering of humanity.
Without detracting in any way
from the awfulness of the cross,
help me to see more clearly
what link there is between the suffering of Jesus and

any suffering which I see around me today.
Help me to realise that any personal suffering
which may come to me
is insignificant compared to yours.
Lord, it is so easy to question you
when suffering, of whatever kind, invades our lives.
When I look out on a world in which
there is so much suffering,
there is always a temptation to doubt your love.
When I am hurting –
whether because of illness, or grief, or loneliness,
or disturbing disappointment, or anxiety -
whatever the nature of it may be,
help me to remember the challenge given to the disciples
to take up their cross and follow their Master.
Remind me that in the midst of it all,
you are there with me –
in Jesus, you too have walked this path of suffering –
yours is a love which dares
to find its expression in suffering.
You are not remote from any troubles I may face,
and even if I angrily blame you,
always reassure me by the power of the cross
that you are closely involved with me.
May that simple, rather cold, unfeeling
statement in the creed,

be transformed into a powerful, challenging call
to accept the warm embrace of your love.

My child, at one time in the history of Christian faith,
what you have said about
the suffering of Jesus, being my suffering,
was judged to be a heresy!
It was declared, "God cannot possibly suffer!"
How wrong they were!
My servant Paul was surely aware of this
when he wrote in his letter to the Church at Corinth,
"God was in Christ, reconciling the world to Himself."
Yes, the suffering you have seen at the cross
was most definitely my suffering also.
I am not remote or unfeeling.
The awful tragic suffering present in the world,
brought on so often by human greed
and selfishness is my suffering also.
I truly am, the Lord who shares the suffering of humanity.

4. "...He descended into hell. On the third day He rose again."

Lord, I have a problem with the first part
of this statement in the Creed.
I am not sure what those who put
these words together really felt we should believe.
If I cling to the traditional concept of Hell,
a place of the damned,
a place of eternal punishment,
(though I do have doubts about that also!)
then, am I really supposed to take it literally,
that the spirit of Jesus descended into such a state?
I think not!
I feel I want to take this as a way of emphasising,
another aspect of the significance of the cross –
that there was no pretence
about the hell of the suffering and rejection –
it was real! –
It was you sharing even the greatest
depths of suffering and despair
which can face a human life.
So Lord, instead of rejecting this statement,
which, I must confess, I am tempted to do,
I take comfort from it –
a comfort which springs from the thought that,

there is no hell which any of us
may have to face in life,
which you do not share
and which you have not entered with us.
On the darkest of days
when I face the depths of despair
you are there with me,
for you have been here yourself.

The key to it all, I see
lies in these wonderful simple words -
"on the third day He rose again"!
Perhaps it is strange that such a
brief, simple statement goes to the heart of it all.
Even in the darkest and most desperate
of experiences which can come,
you reach down to me
with a love which is stronger than death
and you give birth to a hope that can conquer all sorrow.
The guarantee of that
is the glorious triumph of the resurrection
which I gladly celebrate with joy,
not only on Easter Day but on every new day as it dawns.

Of course, I have to face the fact that
the resurrection is undoubtedly
an inexplicable mystery!

One which many would assert
could not possibly have happened -
especially when looked at through modern eyes,
and considered in the context of a world
where, normally, dead people do not come back to life!
But, Lord, I hold fast to the firm assertion of Paul,
expressed in his first letter to the Church in Corinth,
where he declared,
"if Christ has not been raised,
then your faith is a delusion".
So Lord, I gladly hold fast to whatever is
at the heart of the inexplicable Easter event -
Love has been victorious over hatred,
Life has triumphed over death!

My child, your thoughts about
"descended into Hell" should not worry you.
If your reflection on it helps your faith -
as I can see it does —I am happy!
There is no right or wrong view on this —
if different views help the faith of others,
then I am still happy!
It is good for you —
and all my children, to reflect honestly
and allow your reflections
to bring you closer to me.

I understand, too, your thoughts
on the Resurrection.
Of course it cannot be logically explained:
there can never be convincing proof:
you cannot achieve cast iron certainties
about matters of faith.
If there is proof, faith is not necessary.
Continue to hold fast to your faith
and live your life, day by day in the strength of it -
Death has been conquered -
the victory is mine!

5. "...He ascended into heaven, He is seated at the right hand of the Father..."

Lord, I confess to feeling that, probably,
I don't think enough about the significance of this.
I know I have not preached about it very often:
maybe at the back of my mind has been the thought –
how relevant is this to my faith?
I dare to wonder sometimes,
would it not have been better
if the risen Lord Jesus had remained?
Would not that have dispelled on-going doubts
about the reality of the resurrection?
Lord, forgive my speculation, but
could He not have continued
to make appearances to His friends –
both then, and to future generations?

But then, I begin to reflect
on the significance of the words,
"He is seated at the right hand of the Father"
and I take comfort as I realise
that here is a reminder
that the deep interest and love
which Jesus displayed for people
during his life on earth
is carried right to the heart of your very being -

His concern for us and our lives,
is truly and unfailingly, the concern
of you, our loving Heavenly Father.
You convince me of the glorious truth
which would be missing if we had
an ageless Jesus, century after century,
flitting here and there around the world –
the glorious truth that He who shared
completely our humanity, is always with us in Spirit,
responding to our faith.
You convince me that the Ascension
was the change from what is seen
to what is unseen –
from the world of time and space,
with which I am familiar,
to the less familiar, but very real world
which is all around us
but is not tied to time or space –
it is the world which responds to faith.
Lord, it really is all a great mystery!
One which I sometimes feel is
almost too difficult for us to grasp.
Strengthen my faith as I strive
to know you better as the eternal Lord,
powerful over all creation,
unlimited by time, all constraints released,

the unseen Lord who continues
to uphold us by love.

Whatever took place that day on the Mount of Olives
when Jesus departed from his friends,
apparently they walked away from it full of joy.
Enable me, Lord, also to share that joy,
even although I struggle to fathom the mystery –
as by faith I appreciate
that the same Lord Jesus who is eternally,
one with You, is for ever near
and I can know beyond all doubt
that your love is indestructible.

**My child, in a sense, what actually happened
on the Mount of Olives is irrelevant.
It is the truth conveyed by the narrative
which is all important:
I think, from what you have said,
you have grasped that truth:
you have been able to reach out
to the vital, spiritual truth that
you, and all my children, are held
eternally, within my loving embrace
and nothing can ever destroy that.**

6. "...and He will come to judge the living and the dead..."

Lord, 'Judgement' – not a very comfortable topic
on which to reflect!
I am unsure about what the authors of the creed
had in mind when they talked about
judgement of the living –
However I rejoice that Jesus whom we have come
to love, trust and respect, is at the heart
of whatever judgement we have to face.

I accept that my life, day by day,
is under the scrutiny of His loving gaze,
challenging me in all sorts of ways
to live up to His standard.
I know that all too often, I fail
and I am so grateful that I am offered
forgiveness, which I gladly accept.

Judgement of the dead however, seems to be
a topic on which many have very definite opinions!
There are innumerable pages on the internet
which can be accessed under the heading,
"Judgement and God" -
Most seem to emphasise eternal punishment
by you for sinful deeds –

and what is regarded as sinful also varies
from one to another!
The overall image seems to be
one of harsh, uncompromising Judgement by you.
Some even seem to relish the fate
of unrepentant sinners!
Lord, this troubles me!
I certainly don't see your judgement like that at all!

As I try to understand these words of the creed
about judgement of "the dead", I know
I must not ignore any thoughts of judgement which are
expressed in the New Testament –
some of which appear as dire warnings
"to flee from the wrath to come!"
But, Lord, I am convinced that you would not expect me
to take all such words literally:
you would not wish my faith to rest alone on naïve,
unthinking acceptance of an escape route
from the terrors of Hell – whatever that means!

I find the image of Hell, difficult, if not impossible
to reconcile with you, a loving Heavenly Father!
Oh! I know love sometimes has to be harsh or cruel
to be kind – but Hell? For eternity?
Then I think of such situations as the man
who recently murdered

a lovely little girl in a Welsh town –
and even denied the devastated parents
the opportunity to bury her body.
Of course there is a strong feeling
that justice must be done - and that
ultimate justice must be yours!
Lord, there is great mystery here –
as there is with so many matters of faith.
Give me the courage to see beyond
the mystery, to your eternal loving wisdom.

**My child, I am not like some heavenly policeman,
waiting to pounce on the wrong doer!
I am your loving, heavenly Father.
The welfare of all my children is my concern.**

**"judgement of the living" is more a matter of gentle
reprimand and loving guidance in response
to regret and repentance.
There is a story from Japan,
of the student of a religious teacher,
who was caught stealing.
His fellow students requested that he be expelled,
but they were ignored.
The student persisted in his stealing,
so the students presented the master
with an ultimatum – either he dismiss the culprit**

or they would all leave.
The master called them all together and said,
"You are wise brothers: you know right from wrong.
You may go somewhere else to study,
but this poor brother does not even
know right from wrong.
Who will teach him if I do not?
I will keep him here even if you all leave".
The brother who was the thief was so
moved by this that all his desire to steal was gone!"

Reflect on the principle underlying that story
as you try to understand
the mystery of Divine Judgement!
The mystery will in the end become clear - meantime,
rest assured that judgement is safe in my hands!

7. "I believe in the Holy Spirit"

Lord, you must forgive what may well appear
to be rather rambling thoughts about this!
I have no reason to doubt that something
dramatic happened on that Day of Pentecost,
which is reported for us in the early chapters
of the Acts of the Apostles.
Whatever it was, these early Christians
were empowered to be more truly
and enthusiastically, the people of Jesus.
They saw it as the fulfilment
of the promise made to them by Jesus
that your Spirit would come upon
them with power, enabling them
to become effective witnesses to your love.
I am sure that for them, there was
as much an air of mystery about it
as there is for us, as we read about it!
Little did they know that in later generations,
theology would be built around this,
and that there would be bitter disputes
and angry disagreements about
"the Doctrine of the Trinity" which later emerged
as Christians tried to explain
their belief in you as Father, Son and Holy Spirit,

yet still one God!
After all, when they talked about what
had happened, they were only describing,
as best as they could, what their experience had been.

If I go back to the Old Testament,
to the ancient Creation stories,
I find that those who wrote them,
described your creative acts as,
"the Spirit of God was moving over the water".
I notice that in other parts of the Acts of the Apostles,
sometimes instead of saying "Holy Spirit",
Luke, the author, says, "the Spirit of Jesus" -
clearly, both meant the same to him.
he could equally well have said "the Spirit of God"
and conveyed the same important meaning.

If I say that "I believe in the Holy Spirit",
I mean that I believe that you are still active
in your world, encouraging, challenging,
guiding, forgiving, loving, -
making us aware of your presence in a variety of ways.
Forgive me, Lord, for those many times
when I fail to respond to such promptings of your Spirit.

My child, there is no right or wrong way
to give expression to your faith about my Spirit.
Of course you are face to face with mystery.

Mystery will always be at the heart of your faith.
The Apostles, who experienced Pentecost,
described their experience as best as they could,
but of course, as with any spiritual experience,
it defied any full explanation.
From the earliest times,
theologians have tried to probe the mystery,
and offer explanations, but
that is not always helpful
to the simple believer who is endeavouring
to foster a closer relationship with me.
Instead of worrying about trying
to understand "Holy Spirit",
focus instead on experience,
as these early Christians did.
Some Christians give expression to their
awareness of the Spirit's presence
in different ways from others:
be true to your experience,
however it is expressed.
Continue to talk to me:
go on learning to recognise my response to you:
whether that relationship is regarded in
terms of Father, Son or Holy Spirit is immaterial:
it is your relationship with me which is all important.

8. "...the Holy Catholic Church, the communion of saints..."

Lord, how I value the Church! ¬
I don't just mean my local church
where I enjoy such warm fellowship –
I mean the fact that, throughout the world,
there are so many worshippers
who, in common with me,
want to serve and honour you.
They may express their worship
in a way different from me:
they may hold some different views
about basic Christian beliefs,
but we have in common, a love for you -
you are our God, our Lord
who has revealed Himself, especially in Jesus:
we are proud to be known as Christians!

I often feel sad that there is so much
that divides the Church –
different denominations, and
sometimes, within them, more divisions:
disagreements about practice or belief.
And yet the rich variety of ways
in which our faith can be expressed is wonderful -
if only we could learn to tolerate

views different from our own and
realise more fully that the truth has many facets!
But, Lord, I do believe most firmly in
"the Holy Catholic Church" and rejoice in the
universal witness to the faith which is so dear to me.

Lord, as I reflect on "the communion of saints",
maybe I am not very clear about what this means,
but I offer to you these thoughts.
One of the early Christian saints described it as
"a mystical bond uniting
both the living and the dead in
a confirmed hope and love".
I am not sure how far I feel that "mystical bond",
but I do know we owe so much to the
faithful souls who have gone before us.
I don't just mean those whom the Church
has honoured officially as saints:
I think of the words in the letter to the Hebrews
where the writer refers to the "cloud of witnesses",
after he has mentioned a long list of those
regarded as "heroes of faith".
There are millions of others in every generation,
unnamed, but known to you from whom
we have gained so much.

"Communion of saints" also makes me think
of the precious bond which exists
with those I have actually known and loved.
Although no longer with me in the flesh,
there is, nevertheless, a sense of communion,
especially with the one who was,
and still is, most dear to me.
Lord, I give you my deepest thanks,
that death has not robbed me of that treasured bond.

But I do not think of "communion of saints,
only in terms of those who have passed on!
There are also, my fellow Christians
with whom I worship, week by week.
Communion – fellowship with them is also
so precious to me.
Thank you, Lord, for all that I gain
from my Christian brothers and sisters,
whether near, or far off:
whether living or already departed.
In so many and such various ways,
I gain from them, new and different insights into faith –
new ways of expressing my love for you -
Lord, thank you for "the communion of saints".

My child, there is such a rich variety of ways
in which worship is offered – of course there is,

for there are so many different cultures:
yours is only one among many!
People's attitudes
have been shaped by all sorts of factors
and that is part of the glory of the world –
but they are all my children and are within
the embrace of my love.
Don't be disturbed by the differences –
only be sad and concerned when the differences
are allowed to become bitter divisions
which are so destructive.

Do continue to appreciate,
in whatever way is meaningful to you,
the wonder of "communion with saints" and
allow your faith to be enriched and strengthened.
I know there are times when you feel
disheartened and depressed
as you think about the apparent
lack of interest in the Church:
as you worry about dwindling congregations -
and I understand your concern.
But continue to take encouragement
from the words you have mentioned
from the letter to the Hebrews:

" we have this large crowd of witnesses around us.
So then, let us rid ourselves of everything
that gets in the way,
and of the sin which holds on to us so tightly,
and let us run with determination
the race that lies before us.
Let us keep our eyes fixed on Jesus,
on whom our faith depends from beginning to end "

There is so much to be learned from
that "great crowd of witnesses" -
the "heroes of faith" -
the named and unnamed faithful who have gone before,
just as there is from those
who are still with you today.

9."...the forgiveness of sins...".

Lord. In my prayers I often address you as
"forgiving and merciful God".
Perhaps I need to pause, more often than I do,
and reflect on what that means.
It is so easy to take your forgiveness for granted.
I know my faults are many.
In the context of worship,
I find it easy to repeat such words as

"Lord God most merciful,
we confess that we have sinned,
through our own fault, and in common with others,
in thought, word, and deed,
and through what we have left undone.
We ask to be forgiven.
By the power of your Spirit,
turn us from evil to good,
help us to forgive others, and
keep us in your ways of righteousness and love."

As I pray such a prayer
I know that often I am telling myself
that I am not really much of a sinner!
Perhaps I am rather like that young man
who informed Jesus that he had always observed

all the commandments, only to be told
that he was still lacking.
I do take comfort, however,
from also being told that Jesus loved him –
but that doesn't excuse me!
In fact it challenges me,
at least in my better moments,
to examine myself more carefully!

Also in my better moments,
I feel a sense of shame as the line
from the well-known hymn comes to mind –
"He died that we might be forgiven"!
But my thoughts about forgiveness
being dependant on the awful death of Jesus
on the cross are somewhat confused!
I have difficulty with those parts of the
New Testament which suggest that
the death of Jesus was
like a sacrificial offering to you
to appease your anger and
to change you from being a wrathful
and offended God,
into a loving and forgiving Father.
Lord, I cannot think of you like that.
I see you rather, in terms of the father
in Jesus' story which we know as

the parable of the Prodigal Son:
the father who runs to welcome and forgive
his returning, wayward son.
I also find comfort and reassurance
from the words of Paul in his
second letter to the Church at Corinth –
"God was in Christ, reconciling the world to himself".
These words emphasise for me
that you were there at the cross,
telling us of your love and offer of forgiveness.
Lord, I am so glad that,
sinner though I am, you are for me,
the loving, forgiving and merciful Father.

My child, my forgiveness is about restoring
a broken relationship with me -
seeking my forgiveness is not a matter
of "fleeing from the wrath to come"
as many have often made it appear!
It is a sorrowful child responding
to the Father's love –
a love which was demonstrated at the cross.
The sufferings of Jesus were my sufferings also.
I know there is great mystery here
which probably defies human understanding.
I know that there are other ways
in which this has been expressed -

even in the New Testament,
but above all, when you talk about
my forgiveness, you are talking about my love.
Remember words from the prayer of Jesus
in John's Gospel when He prayed
for the unity of His followers:
"I pray that they may all be one,
Father ... just as you are in me and I am in you."
I was very much in Him at the cross,
as at any other time.
I did not need some perfect sacrifice
to persuade me to show forgiveness -
love does not work like that!
True love dares to suffer
to find its full expression -
True love wants to forgive –
True love longs for reconciliation.
When you address me as
"forgiving and merciful God"
you are reaching out to me, whose great love
is already reaching out to you.

10. "the resurrection of the body, and the life everlasting."

Lord as I reflect on what may happen after death,
I have great difficulty with, at least,
the first part of this statement in the Creed.
Am I really supposed to take it literally
and believe that the body
which has been either buried or cremated
will, at some time in the future,
be put together again?
Surely not!
But I do want to cling to the idea
that death is not the end.
As I grieve for my beloved who passed away,
I cannot believe that the one who was
so dear to me has now become nothing –
only a treasured memory!
Nor can I believe great characters
such as Handel or Mozart, who have
inspired millions with their music,
and countless others like Martin Luther King,
or Nelson Mandela, whom it
would be a joy to know,
have all been obliterated into nothingness.
Lord, as I try, from time to time, to imagine

the nature of life beyond this one,
the mystery of it all does fill me
with confusing doubts.
While I cannot subscribe to belief in
the resurrection of the body,
I still must cling to the strong hope that
the personality lives on
and even after death,
precious fellowship is reborn
with those who have gone before.

The confusing doubts refuse
to leave me completely -
but, counteracting these doubts,
you keep challenging me to hold fast to
the Christian hope, expressed so well
in the words of the Apostle Paul -

"I am persuaded, that neither death, nor life,
nor angels, nor principalities, nor powers,
nor things present, nor things to come,
nor height, nor depth, nor any other creature,
shall be able to separate us from
the love of God, which is in Christ Jesus our Lord."

My child, of course it is mystery!
Life itself is a mysterious adventure
in which the future is hidden from you:

so it must be with what lies beyond.
Reflect again on the words of Jesus:

Do not be worried and upset,"
"Believe in God and believe also in me.
There are many rooms in my Father's house,
and I am going to prepare a place for you.
I would not tell you this if it were not so.
And after I go and prepare a place for you,
I will come back and take you to myself,
so that you will be where I am.

Reflect also on the words which Paul
quoted to the Corinthians from the Prophet Isaiah,
"Eye has not seen, nor ear heard,
neither have entered into the heart of man,
the things which God has prepared
for those that love him."

Cling to your belief in "the life everlasting" –
continue to trust me -
the mystery will eventually be revealed:
trust me;
the future is safe with me.